PHOTOGRAPHIC MEMORIES
OF
EAST ANGLIA

A Further Selection

Front cover picture:
From the Pier, Southwold 1906 (56829)

Above:
The Quay at Great Yarmouth in 1908 (60652)

FRANCIS FRITH AND HIS UNIQUE ARCHIVE

In 1860, Francis Frith, the Quaker son of a Chesterfield cooper, was 38 years old. He had already sold a massive grocery business he had built up, for a small fortune. Like Livingstone and Stanley, Frith was fired with a romantic Wanderlust, and the Victorian deep passion for travelling and exploring. Between 1857 and '59 he made several pioneering photographic journeys to remote regions of the Nile that brought him considerable fame.

After his marriage in 1860, he confined his wanderings a little closer to home and began a series of photo trips around Britain. His aim was to make his pictures available to the greatest number of people possible - life was hard and drab for millions of Victorians, and Frith believed his 'view souvenirs' of seaside resorts, beauty spots and town and village scenes would help keep their rare days out alive in their memories. He was right: by 1890 he had created the largest photographic publishing company in the world!

As well as thousands of views of high streets around Britain, Frith's growing archive included beautiful scenes of leafy glades, dusty lanes, rocks and coastlines, and the boats and riversides, beloved of Victorian wanderers like Jerome K Jerome - whose 'Three Men in a Boat' had struck a strong chord with the public.

Life in the Frith family was never dull. The family went with him on many trips, and the highlights were recorded by his wife, Mary Ann, in her journal. In 1872 she tells of a relaxing three week expedition to Ilfracombe in North Devon. Whilst such trips may have been something of a holiday for his wife and children, Francis Frith found no time to put his feet up. He was up and down the coast photographing Barnstaple and Lynton, hiring carters to carry him out to remote locations, and boatsmen to row him round the bay to view and photograph spectacular cliff formations.

After Francis Frith died in 1898 his sons carried on the business for many years with great success, specialising in postcards and other prints. So impressive is the archive he started that **The Financial Times** called it *'a unique and priceless record of English life in the last century'*.

PHOTOGRAPHIC MEMORIES

OF

EAST ANGLIA

A Further Selection

THE FRANCIS FRITH COLLECTION

This edition published by
The Francis Frith Collection exclusively for
Selectabook Ltd., Roundway, Devizes,
Wiltshire SN10 2HR

Picture compilation and text by Jenny de Gex

First Published in 1996

© The Francis Frith Collection

ISBN 1 85937 024 1

Printed in Italy by Imago Publishing

Reproductions of all the photographs in this book
are available as framed or mounted prints from
The Francis Frith Collection at the address below.
Please quote the town, full title and negative number
shown in brackets.

The Francis Frith Collection
The Old Rectory, Bimport, Shaftesbury, Dorset SP7 8AT
Tel: 01747 855669 Fax: 01747 855065

Contents

FELIXSTOWE. Popular as an Edwardian seaside resort, Felixstowe has grown up on a promontory where the estuary of the rivers Stour and Orwell meet the sea. The 20 foot wide concrete promenade was begun in 1902, and stretches for two miles, with a pier extending half a mile at the mid-point. There were grand hotels, but these are now office blocks, and despite the industrial encroachment today from one of the country's largest sea container terminals at the docks, it can never totally lose its feel of Edwardian resort.

Right: Spa Pavilion, Felixstowe 1909 (62005) Inside a typically iron-spanned Edwardian pavilion, people can be seen no doubt taking their afternoon tea, while the gracious background of stone urns and hydrangeas makes a suitable setting for a gentle stroll.

Above: East Beach, Felixstowe 1899 (44514) Although mainly off a shingle beach, the bathing was considered safe, although one had to be hardy to brave the rigours of the North Sea in the first place. Small wonder that many preferred to walk for their health, breathing in the fresh easterly breeze.

Top: Beach, Felixstowe 1907 (58958) The south facing shingly bay, with a wide beach, provided safe bathing. Ladies sensibly wore their hats as protection against the sun's damaging rays, to keep their complexions pale. **Above: The Pier, Felixstowe 1906** (54640) Everything is not as it seems in this picture. The car, the boats and the groups of people are actually from other photographs, and have been cut out and added to an otherwise empty beach scene. It was common practice with many early photographic studios to update (or spice up) their older pictures in this way. Can you spot the joins?

Above: The Beach, Felixstowe 1904
(51254) The beach is divided into
sections by groynes or breakwaters
stretching into the sea. Behind are
lined up hundreds of wooden bathing
huts that can be hired for the season
or by the swim.

**Left: The Gardens and Cliff Hotel,
Felixstowe 1907** (58965) An afternoon
in the sun in the cliff-top gardens
beside one of the town's grandest
hotels, the Cliff.

**Opposite above: From the Pier,
Felixstowe 1906** (54637)
A private railway ran from Ipswich to
Beach and Pier stations opening in
1877, Town Station opened in 1898,
thus bringing thousands to the
seaside.

**Opposite below: The Docks,
Felixstowe 1907** (58986) Around the
corner on the Orwell, the docks,
previously used for the shipping of
grain from local mills, are now an
important ferry port.

PSWICH. The county town of East Suffolk, it is hard to believe this was once the largest port between the Thames and the Humber. Its origin is due to its position at the mouth of the river Orwell's estuary, Gipeswic, meaning wic, a town, and gip, a corner of the mouth. The Vikings landed here in the 10th century, indeed priceless treasure was found from the Sutton Hoo Ship Burial, only about twenty miles away. Trading mainly in cloth and grain, and bringing coal from the north of England, the harbour provided an important focus and Daniel Defoe remembers seeing 'perhaps two hundred sail of ships'.

Top: Butter Market, Ipswich 1921 (70404) Medieval in origin, the Butter Market is today a bustling shopping centre, continuing its early function of a thriving marketplace. **Above: Mill, Ipswich 1909** (61998) On the quieter reaches of the river, away from the industrialized port, sailing can still be a pleasurable pastime. **Opposite: Lock Gates, Ipswich** (70413) These magnificent sailing barges transported the trade of the city to London and back. Although a rare sight today, they can still be seen as holiday craft along the river estuaries of East Anglia, or racing on special occasions. The Dutch influence is obvious.

Opposite above: Ancient House, Ipswich 1921 (70399) The pride of Ipswich, dating from the 15th century, the pargetting or plastermoulding on the outside is Restoration, symbolizing four continents, as the fifth had yet to be discovered.

Opposite below: The White Horse, Ipswich 1893 (32202) Mr Pickwick apparently had many adventures at the Great White Horse, a well-known inn of the 19th century, whose sign can just be seen to the right. Dickens was in Ipswich in 1835.

Above: Tavern Street, Ipswich 1896 (37306) In a city known for brewing, it is only appropriate that one of its early medieval streets be named after its taverns. The Town Hall, to the right, was built in mid-Victorian times in 'Venetian' style.

Left: River Orwell, Ipswich 1921 (70414) Due to the importance of nearby wool towns such as Lavenham, the main business was exporting cloth and wheat from the vast wheatfields, stored in granaries along the docks. Colliery ships would transport coal from the north of England, thereby supplying London and the south.

FLATFORD MILL. The definitive images of East Anglia were painted by one of its most famous sons, John Constable, in the early 19th century. Born at East Bergholt Hall, his paintings of Dedham Vale, the Stour valley and surrounding countryside are some of the finest examples of British landscape painting. His father owned a mill at Flatford and this was to prove one of the key images of Constable's art, as the subject or setting for numerous studies between 1811 and 1816.

Right: Willy Lott's Cottage, Flatford Mill 1906 (57554) Willy Lott was a tenant farmer who was born and lived for a reputed eighty-eight years in this house owned by Constable's father. Constable painted many studies of the whole house, and the right hand part is represented in the celebrated painting 'The Hay-Wain'. All that is missing from this photograph is the carter and his cart standing in the millstream, with the dog looking on.

Above: Flatford Mill, Suffolk 1907 (57551) The mill buildings seen across the water with the trees and their reflections balancing the scene, often with figures in the foreground, made perfect composition practice for the young artist. Constable usually painted the building from the location. The building is now owned by the National Trust and is a field study centre.

Top: Bridge Cottage, Flatford Mill 1907 (57552) This photograph could almost be a study for Constable's paintings of 'Boys Fishing' which show this same rickety wooden bridge. The scene is peaceful and timeless almost a hundred years later captured by the camera rather than on canvas. The thatched cottage has been restored and houses an exhibition about Constable. **Above: The Guildhall, Hadleigh 1922** (71975) A lasting testament to the medieval wealth of the wool towns grouped around the Suffolk border, this fine example of a half-timbered Cloth Hall or Guild Hall dates from around 1430, and is notable for its two overhanging upper storeys.

Above: Church Street, Hadleigh c1950
(H2008) One of the largest churches in Suffolk, St Mary's has an elegant lead spire rising to 135 feet, and one of the oldest Angelus Bells in the country, some 600 years old. A Danish leader, Guthrum, who was defeated by King Alfred and subsequently converted to Christianity, was buried here.

Left: Deanery Gateway, Hadleigh 1921
(71976) This fine gateway dates from 1495 and is made of red brick, seemingly a small replica of the gatehouse to Oxburgh Hall in Norfolk. It was the entrance to a deanery palace that has since been demolished.

Above: The Village, Kersey c1955 (K136027) Kersey is one of the most picturesque Suffolk villages, hidden in a steep-sided valley. Except for traces of modern life such as wires or street signs, one could be in a period film set for medieval Britain, so unchanged does it remain. The typical weavers' cottages are half-timbered or of colour washed plaster.

Right: The Ford and Church, Kersey c1955 (K136008) The ford runs into a tributary of the river Brett, in whose valley Kersey lies. Used as a cart wash, the stream crosses the village, and was undoubtedly useful in its former days of cloth manufacturing. Kersey gave its name to a hardwearing broadcloth, mentioned in Shakespeare.

SUDBURY. The largest of the wool and weaving towns in this western part of Suffolk, Sudbury nestles in a loop of the river Stour. Important as a market town for the neighbourhood, it was also the birthplace and home of the 18th-century painter Thomas Gainsborough. Although he loved to paint trees and landscapes, it was for portraiture that he later became known, which he practiced young by painting wealthy patrons while living in Sudbury and Ipswich, before moving away to Bath and London. His house, formerly a 16th-century inn, is now a museum.

Top: Market Hill, Sudbury 1900 (45068) Sudbury was a port on the River Stour of great importance until the coming of the railways. Barges transported goods from Ipswich and beyond, and thus trade was prosperous. Consequently, the market place was busy and held considerable importance both for fresh produce and farming implements such as can be seen here. **Above: The Exchange, Sudbury 1895** (35467) The buildings in the centre of Sudbury were mainly Georgian, but the shopfronts have not always been too kindly adapted.

Above: Market Hill, Sudbury 1900
(45067) The church of St Peter's dominating Market Hill was a grand building, with a traceried roof panelled in blue and gold, carved 16th-century chairs, and a 15th-century embroidery that was formerly used for special funerals. It is now redundant and used only for concerts. A statue of Gainsborough now stands outside the church, looking down over the town.

Left: Brundon Mill, Sudbury 1895
(35487) The willow-fringed banks of the river make a picturesque setting, but this typical Suffolk mill just outside Sudbury at Brundon would still have been in practical use, as the horse and cart waits to transport freshly milled sacks of flour.

AVENHAM. One of the most perfect surviving examples of a medieval village in Britain, virtually every street is composed of beautiful 14th to 16th-century thatched, rough plaster or half-timbered buildings, and often a combination of all three. The great oak timbers and clay and wattle fillings are typical of Suffolk architecture, and there are no straight lines as beams and gable ends curve and tilt in irregular ways. Timber was scarce and costly, only affordable by the rich: this alone is proof of Lavenham's former wealth.

Top: The Church Porch, Lavenham c1955 (L21002) The lasting monument to the wealth of the local wool merchants is all too apparent in the lavish and ornate decoration of this fine church porch. The church is a splendid example of the Perpendicular, the flint bell tower standing 141 foot high. **Above: Lavenham 1904** (51180) The Guildhall is the most important building in Lavenham, after the church. Built in the 1520s by the Guild regulating wool production, it is now owned by the National Trust and has been restored to house a museum telling the story of the wool trade.

Above: Long Melford Hall 1895 (35492)
Close to Sudbury, the village of Long
Melford has a three-mile long main
street, best experienced from the south.
From a wide and gracious High Street
lined with Georgian and earlier timber-
framed houses, it opens out to a large
green with the walls of Melford Hall on
one side and a magnificent hilltop
church of Holy Trinity, contemporary
with Lavenham. Melford Hall was built
in the 16th century on land that had
been a deer park for the abbots of Bury
St Edmunds. The Parker family lived
here since acquiring the Hall in the 18th
century, but it is now National Trust and
open to the public .

Left: Callis Street, Clare c1955
(C512004) Typical Suffolk plastered
buildings form a backdrop to a small
gathering of what seem to us vintage
cars, yet are only forty years old. Clare
was named after the brightness and
clarity of the River Stour to the south.

NEWMARKET. Today a road sign warns visitors approaching Newmarket of 'Racehorses for 5 miles'. The undisputed centre of Britain's horseracing and bloodstock breeding, it has more thoroughbred racehorses than anywhere else in the world. James I organized the first recorded race in 1619, having been a visitor for hawking or tilting or harecoursing. The annual yearling sales are all-important: today horse transport is mainly by specially fitted road transporters, but in the days of rail travel, there was a special station for the horses' reception.

Right: Horses at Exercise, Newmarket 1929 (81964) The countryside around Newmarket boasts a dense concentration of stud farms and racing stables. Trainers of classic race winners abound in the neighbourhood. A daily ritual for the stable lads and jockeys is to ride out and exercise their precious charges on the 'gallops'.

Above: High Street, Newmarket 1922 (71912) Less than twenty years after this photograph, ten bombs fell on this High Street during the Second World War. The town is set on this, one of the most ancient roads in England. It is home to the Jockey Club, which is housed in an impressive building in this street, next door to the National Horse Racing Museum.

Above: Angel Hotel, Bury St Edmunds 1929 (81945) Known locally just as the shortened Bury, the town is still relatively unspoiled, and boasts some fine Georgian buildings. Angel Hill and Angel Square are at the heart of these, lined with handsome Regency and Georgian buildings. Mr Pickwick had one of his many adventures at the Angel Hotel, now immortalised by Dickens.

Left: Abbey Gate, Bury St Edmunds 1922 (71956) The first monastery at Bury dated from AD630. Subsequently, the Danish King Canute, after conquering England in 1016, converted to Christianity and gave substantial lands to the monastery. Thereafter a Benedictine abbey flourished, making a focal point to the town. The Abbey is now in ruins but this massive Norman Gate survives.

WOODBRIDGE. An air of quiet sophistication pervades Woodbridge, tinged strongly with the salt of the sea air from the nearby Deben estuary. A former sea port, the water traffic these days is purely for pleasure or sport. A handsome town, with elegant Georgian buildings intermingled with more traditional Suffolk vernacular cottages in their bright limewashed colours. Former notable inhabitants included the translator of the Rubaiyat of Omar Khayam, and writer of *The Golden Bough*, Edward Fitzgerald.

Right: Woodbridge 1906 (53495) Behind the sailing barge can be seen the Tide Mill, an 18th-century clapboard mill, which used the tide to drive grinding machinery. This has now been restored to working order.

Above: The Beach, Woodbridge 1898 (42773) The waterfront seems slightly apart from the town, yet provided hours of simple pleasure for children and adults alike, then as now. Wading birds are content in this natural habitat, and on a walk along the riverbank of a summer's evening one can see a wide variety.

Top: The Thoroughfare, Woodbridge 1894 (33374) Many original Victorian shop fronts can still be seen today in the now pedestrianised Thoroughfare, which caters for most specialist needs. **Above: Boat Station, Woodbridge 1894** (33372) In the 19th century, the railway station was placed near the river, amidst boatyards and on the edge of the natural harbour provided by the river. Earlier, in the mid 17th century, some 350 ships were registered here, and shipyards built seagoing vessels as well as warships. The building tradition continues for pleasure craft and yachts. **Overleaf: The Beach, Woodbridge 1898** (42772)

Above: The Castle, Framlingham 1910
(82078) Nine miles inland from
Woodbridge, Framlingham is
overlooked by the massive ruins of a
13th-century curtain-walled castle,
with thirteen towers. Based on the
castles seen by Crusaders, it was the
stronghold of the Dukes of Norfolk
until the 17th century.

Left: Market Hill, Framlingham 1909
(62028) Memorials to the Howards,
the family of the Dukes of Norfolk, are
to be seen in the church, with many
accompanying bloodthirsty tales of
beheading in the times of Henry VIII
and Elizabeth I. This extraordinary
example of tree surgery continues
fashions begun in more formalised
gardens, for training hedges.

**Opposite above: Market Place,
Framlingham c1950** (FLH003)

**Opposite below: Market Hill,
Framlingham c1950** (FLH005)

ALDEBURGH. The Aldeburgh shown in these photographs is the simple seaside place that so attracted one of its more famous inhabitants, the composer Benjamin Britten in the mid-20th century. It has brought an influx of seasonal visitors for its international music festival founded in 1948. Nonetheless, the simple fishing port with its shingle beach and seafront remains relatively unchanged. An Aldeburgh poet, George Crabbe, wrote a portrait of the town in 1810, *The Borough*, which formed the libretto for Britten's opera, Peter Grimes.

Right: Slaughden Quay, Aldeburgh 1894 (33365) Back from a long fishing trip, the crew of WF 63 are securing the mast and spars and clearing the decks before going ashore. A small boy is riding the shallows in a makeshift punt.

Above: High Street, Aldeburgh 1894 (33362) Wattle-and-daub cottages were rebuilt in brick as Aldeburgh gradually developed as a watering-place. This wide part of the street sees a unique event every summer: on the last night of the Carnival, thousands gather in a procession carrying paper lanterns through the town, led by a band and a Carnival Queen, to watch a firework display over the sea, sitting on upturned boats on the shingle beach. Shops and houses hold a competition for the most imaginatively decorated window.

Top: The Lifeboat 'Winchester', Aldeburgh 1903 (50426) Despite wild and tempestuous seas which can hit the beach in easterly gales, the lifeboat has never failed to launch when called. **Above: The Esplanade, Aldeburgh 1984** (33355) The beach has many boats or 'punts' belonging to the local fishermen, who go out in search of herring and sprats. George Crabbe depicted the Aldeburgh inhabitants as ' a wild amphibious race'. **Overleaf: The Beach, Aldeburgh 1906** (56817)

Above: The Mill House, Aldeburgh 1908 (62012) The remains of an old windmill has been converted to make a highly original seaside house. *Alde burh* means old fort, and this strange house has something of the air of an ancient fortification about it, even though modern.

Left: The Golf House, Aldeburgh 1896 (38673) The Golf Club was founded by the husband of the eminent pioneer doctor, Elizabeth Garrett Anderson, who later became mayor of Aldeburgh in 1907.

Opposite above: The Esplanade, Aldeburgh 1896 (38668) Victorian and Edwardian architecture stands side by side with 1920s seaside houses. Discerning holidaymakers built their summer villas here long before its more fashionable days. Streets and alley ways have evocative names such as Neptune's Alley.

Opposite below: Parade and Beach, Aldeburgh 1929 (82969)

THORPENESS. This unusual resort was the creation of Stuart Ogilvie, in memory of his mother. Work began in 1910 with various additions until the late 1920s, from which period most of these photographs date. The Meare was a kind of oversize village pond, designed for the pleasures of safe boating without fear of tide or current.

Right: The Park, Thorpeness 1929 (82985) Neo-Tudor cottages were built, and other holiday homes in a more modern style, to found a then-original holiday village, which must have been quite an innovation at the time.

Above: The Lake, Thorpeness 1929 (82987) Quietly pottering on the water amidst the reeds, combining the natural vegetation of the area with the man-made lake or Meare as it is known. **Opposite: The House in the Clouds, Thorpeness c1955** (T38012) An 1803 windmill was moved from nearby Aldringham, and used to pump water to supply the newly-created village into a folly of a tower which stood 85 heet high and was disguised as a clapboard house.

Right: Saxmundham 1929 (82949) Six miles north-west of Aldeburgh, Saxmundham was much altered by the coming of the railway as the town became a centre for iron working and engineering. A fine example of local iron work can be seen in the wrought iron railing in the foreground.

Below: Leiston Abbey 1922 (72584) The Abbey, founded in the 12th century, is in a romantic setting amidst wheatfields. Now owned by a Trust for the benefit of young musicians, it holds study courses and summer schools.

Top: The Village and Church, Blythburgh 1895 (36881) Dramatically rising out of the flat marshland, the magnificent church of Holy Trinity dominates the skyline for miles around. Tidal waters almost lap at the feet of the 83 foot tower. Mostly dating from the mid 15th century, the tiebeam roof has superb examples of carved wooden angels and is painted in decorative medieval style with heraldic and symbolic emblems. The angels' wings were damaged in the Civil War by Cromwell's soldiers, who also stabled their horses here.
Above: The Beach, Walberswick 1892 (29934) This small riverside harbour offers views across the saltmarshes to Southwold.

SOUTHWOLD. With cliffs, a long sandy beach, a harbour and its own brewery, Southwold is an ideal holiday resort for 'discriminating persons'. A hundred years after these photographs, it still retains the air of a Victorian bathing-place. The buildings are a mixture of Georgian pantiles or brick, amidst colour-washed fishermen's cottages. A main street and a handful of side streets open onto delightful open greens, offering wide views out over marshes and heaths.

Right: East Green, Southwold 1893 (32184) This dominating landmark of a white lighthouse looms as a reminder of Southwold's prominent coastal position, an essential beacon to the fishermen out upon merciless seas.

Above: The Common, Southwold 1899 (44502) Taking the word Common very literally, these cows think it means for them as well. In the background is the tower of the 15th-century church of St Edmund's, one of Suffolk's most justly celebrated churches, which has a figure of 'Southwold Jack' striking a bell to mark the hours and the times of services. **Opposite: From the Pier, Southwold 1906** (56829) Although invented in the 18th century, bathing machines were still in use at the turn of the 20th century. What would the Victorians and Edwardians think of today's beach wear and behaviour one wonders - probably not amused.

Above: Mill on the Common, Southwold 1893 (32191) A terrible fire almost totally destroyed the town in 1659, and it is said the grouping around different greens is an attempt to prevent a recurrence. These boys are in front of what looks like the markings of a grass tennis court.

Left: Market, Southwold 1896 (38627) Fish is often to be found deliciously fresh at markets by the sea. There was hope in Edwardian times of a revival of the town's herring industry, as curing began again in 1908. Alas, the main industry went to Yarmouth and Lowestoft, but Southwold preserved its charm as a result. The goat cart was a novel way to carry children around as a special seaside treat.

Opposite above: The Common, Southwold 1896 (38629) Another angle of the Common, with bemused tiny tots: smile please!

Opposite below: The Beach, Southwold 1906 (56834) Panamas, straw hats and even a proper little boy's sailor suit present a fashion parade for Edwardian children.

L OWESTOFT. Extensive bombing during the Second World War ruined most of the old town, which for years had been at the forefront of the herring fishing industry. Lowestoft is a mixture of seaside resort and fishing port, the latter at its real heart. Kipper-curing houses and net-drying frames would still have been in use at the time of these photographs, as would the Lowestoft Trawlers, ketch-rigged and capable of holding the sea in all weathers.

Top: High Lighthouse, Lowestoft 1921 (71705) The Upper Lighthouse stands on the site of Britain's first ever lighthouse, powerd originally by a coal fire. Around it are alley ways known as 'scores', once lined with fishermen's cottages with smokehouses attached. **Above: Yacht Basin, Lowestoft 1896** (37939) The harbour, with twin lighthouses, was built in 1827-31, and although initially handling commercial goods, then became a yacht basin used by the Royal Lowestoft Yacht Club.

Above: Lowestoft 1922 (72506) Winds blowing straight off the North Sea can cause untold damage, hence the beach is safely shored up to prevent further encroachment from the sea's ravages.

Left: South Pier Pavilion, Lowestoft 1921 (71694) South Town is the resort part of Lowestoft, and was developed from 1847 onwards. An attempt to make the North as popular never succeeded.

Above: Lowstoft 1919 (69309) Soon after the end of the First Wold War, Britain was slowly coming back to life. These boats moored in the tranquillity of the river seem mainly pleasure craft, but Lowestoft was still important for its fishing industry.

Left: Fritton Lake, Lowestoft c1890 (L105501)

Opposite top: Lowestoft 1922 (72497) This couple are seemingly oblivious of the phoographer behind them, busily recording the passing fashions and fads of the 1920s. The patriotism of the average town is something we find hard to understand today: the Union Jack was flown at the slghtest excuse.

Opposite below: Lowestoft 1887 (19886) The south part of Lowestoft was the chief bathing and holiday resort, known as South Town. It boasted some massive hotels, such as the Royal built in 1848.

ECCLES. On the edge of the Broads, built on rising ground above the River Waveney, sailing is still popular here. Private staithes and moorings lie at the end of gardens stretching to the water's edge. In the days when it was still a thriving port, wherries plied their way up and down river, transporting goods from the sea ports inland.

Right: Market Place, Beccles 1894 (33334) A thriving market town, before road transport, most produce came to Beccles by ship, or was exchanged in the local market place. By the 1890s the bicycle was already a form of popular transport, as can be seen by these left outside the local inn. The bell tower of St Michael's rises 97 feet above the scene.

Above: From the Marshes, Beccles 1894 (33332) In the distance can be seen St Michael's church, with its detached bell tower. The porch is finely decorated, although the church itself is plain. The main claim to fame is that Nelson's parents were married there.

Top: Market Place, Bungay 1951 (B617026) The lead-covered Butter Cross to the right was built in 1689, after a fire nearly destroyed the town. The figure on the top represents Justice. The buildings around are fine examples of the town's Georgian prosperity. These trucks look almost like toys in comparison to the vast trailers we know today. **Above: Oulton Broad, Suffolk 1886** (19876) The southernmost of the Broadlands network, Oulton Broad was and is a popular place for small boat sailing. It now has a small museum with displays on Lowestoft's Porcelain factory, local history and archaeology.

H ARLESTON. Only a mile over the Suffolk border, Harleston is one of Norfolk's frontier towns. A pleasing market town on the north bank of the river Waveney, there are elegant Georgian houses and early shop fronts still to be seen. The old parish church is about a mile from the town at Redenhall, now part of Harleston. The tower has dramatic vertical stripes of flint and stone, but in 1872 the Victorians built their own church in the town centre.

Right: The Thoroughfare, Harleston c1955 (H305005) On the right can be seen the elaborate wrought-iron inn sign for the Swan Hotel, which has an elegant 18th-century facade. One of two of the finest Georgian houses in the town, the other, Candlers House, was rated by Pevsner one of the best in the country.

Above: The Market Place, Harleston c1955 (H305002) The market must be at the beginning or end of the day as things seem none too busy for the single stallholder. The hotel bears another decorative and imaginative piece of wrought-iron work in its sign, as can be seen more clearly in the picture opposite of the silhouetted magpie. **Opposite: The Thoroughfare, Harleston c1955** (H305021)

DISS. Taking its name from the Old English *dic*, meaning a ditch or pond, this is most appropriate for Diss is built around a six-acre mere or lake. This unique feature makes it look like a large village around an extra large village pond. It is altogether a most attractive country town, with some half-timbered medieval and also Georgian buildings.

Right: Mere Street, Diss 1925
(77325) Mere Street opens out at the southern end into a public park, where water birds come to feed. Note the classic sign of His Master's Voice hanging outside a shop which presumably sold new-fangled gramophone records?

Below: St Nicholas Street, Diss c1955
(D32010) On the left is the Greyhound Inn, which dates from the 15th century.

Above: The Mere, Diss 1925 (77329)
Water fowl thrive here, and the more
adventurous have been known to go on
expeditions into the town, to the
surprise of passing shoppers.

Left: Market Place, Diss c1955
(D32012) The Market Place where
markets were regularly held has raised
pavements and a Victorian Shambles.
The church of St Mary the Virgin in the
background has been much restored. A
poet and tutor to Henry VIII, John
Skelton, was Rector of Diss, but was
apparently more fitted for the stage
than the pulpit.

THETFORD. Just two miles over the Suffolk border, Thetford may have been the tribal capital of the Iceni, the people who, under Boudicca nearly succeeded in driving the Romans out of Britain in AD 60. Iron Age defences survive around the town, and a Norman motte was built to guard the place where the prehistoric Icknield Way crosses the Little Ouse.

Right: Town Bridge, Thetford 1929 (81836) The rivers Thet and Little Ouse run parallel to each other, and Regency Houses line the banks of each. The capital of Breckland, Thetford is both a medieval and Georgian town. The most important writer born in Thetford was Thomas Paine, author of *The Rights of Man*.

Above: Mill Head, Thetford 1929 (81834) Thetford Mill occupies an island between the two rivers, Thet and Little Ouse. With their propensity to found communities beside water, the Benedictines built a monastery at Thetford in 1020, which came into the possession of nuns in the 12th century. Although these settlements often had their own fish ponds, these smooth flowing waters must have yielded plenty of fresh fish.

Above: Market Place, Thetford 1929 (81830) In the Market Place, these bystanders stare intrigued at the camera. A strange story lies contained in the nearby Guildhall, which houses portraits given to the town by a local antiquary, Prince Duleep Singh. He also donated a building in White Hart Street, the Ancient House. The Prince's father came to England as a child and enchanted Queen Victoria. Nonetheless she forced him to hand over the priceless Koh-i-Noor diamond, and exiled him as ruler of the Punjab. His son, who lived near Thetford, was a knowledgeable historian. Behind the Guildhall were the Cage and Stocks dating from 1581.

Left: St Cuthbert's Church, Thetford 1921 (70915) Little of the original building remains, as total rebuilding was needed after the tower fell in 1851.

KING'S LYNN. The king in question was Henry VIII, who changed the name from 'Lynn Episcopi', as it was known until the Reformation. Built on the east bank of the Ouse, about two miles from the Wash, the town has a distinctively Flemish flavour, similar to market towns in Belgium. All thrived on trade within the Hanseatic League, of the North Sea and Baltic countries. There are many things worth visiting, notably the Guildhall, with flint flushwork, and the Renaissance Customs House. St George's Hall is the oldest theatre in England.

Right: South Gate, King's Lynn 1925 (78716) The South Gate is the only town gate left, for the East Gate was demolished in 1800. Last rebuilt in 1520, it stands on London Road, proudly boasting turrets and battlements. Nearby streets indicate the line of the old wall.

Above: Norfolk Street, King's Lynn 1891 (28769) Hilaire Belloc approached King's Lynn from the Ouse in 1908. 'You can see the past effect of ownership and individuality in King's Lynn as clearly as you can catch afection or menace in a human voice. The outward expression is most manifest, and to pass in and out along the lanes in front of the old houses inspires in one precisly those emotions which are aroused by a human crowd'.

Top: River Bridge, King's Lynn 1925 (78719) A 20th-century bridge spans the river that previously carried produce from the East Midlands and the rest of East Anglia to Lynn's busy port, where warehouses and merchants' houses lined the quays. **Above: The Quay, King's Lynn 1898** (40893) In 1722, Daniel Defoe visited King's Lynn and wrote of 'the vast advantages in trade' to be gained from its extensive system of waterborne transport by navigable waterways 'whereby six counties wholly, and three counties in part' could be supplied with imported merchandise.

Above: High Street, King's Lynn 1891
(28770) With the coming of the railways
King's Lynn lost trade yet there is much
evidence of its past prosperity.

Left: Nelson Street, King's Lynn 1908
(60025) Curving at the eastern end,
Nelson street follows the line of the
original harbour. The 15th-century jettied
Hampton Court has a cannon ball fired
by the Parliamentarians when besieging
Lynn: although the Royalists held out
bravely against 4000 horse and foot, they
eventually had to capitulate.

Right: Town Hall, King's Lynn 1925
(78715A) Originally the Hall of the
Trinity Guild, this handsome
building of chequered flint and
stone was built half a millennium
ago. Here are kept the town's
Charters and the Red Register, one
of the oldest paper books in
existence, containing 13th-century
municipal records.

**Below: The Honest Lawyer Inn,
King's Lynn 1925** (78717) This pub
is situated close to the South Gate.
Its name must have prompted many
a debate on the theme is there such
a thing as an honest lawyer?

HUNSTANTON. One of the few places on the east coast that faces west, this ensures fine sunsets over the Wash. Old Hunstanton is slightly inland, with quiet lanes and creepered cottages. New Hunstanton comes up to the cliffs and down to the sea, centred around a green at the centre of which is an ancient cross. The transformation into a popular resort began in the 1860s at the initiative of Hamon le Strange of Hunstanton Hall, much boosted by the arrival of the railway in 1862.

Right: From the Pier, Hunstanton 1907 (58897) The pier, built in the 1870s, has since disappeared, but it was often the objective of a healthy stroll in the bracing sea air. These fine gentlemen seem very dapper with their gleaming white spats.

Above: The Lighthouse, Hunstanton 1907 (58899) The 1830 lighthouse stands on top of the sixty-foot cliffs, famous among geologists for their curious formation with a band of red chalk coming between the brown and yellow of the base and the white chalk of the top. Next to the lighthouse are the ruins of St Edmund's chapel: legend has it that before becoming king of East Anglia, he was nearly shipwrecked here, and founded the chapel as thanksgiving for his escape from drowning.

Top: Cross and Pier, Hunstanton 1921 (71021) Small boys amuse themselves with cricket at this vantage point close to the Pier.
Above: The Green and Pier, Hunstanton 1927 (79723) The forerunner of today's motorised ice-cream vans, miraculously always to be found close to some tourist spot or vantage point, were these horse-drawn ice-cream carts.

Above: The Pier, Hunstanton 1921 (71033) These children are searching rock pools at low tide for any crabs or shrimps that might be lurking there.

Left: The Beach and Cliffs, Hunstanton 1927 (79735) The different stripes in the rocks of the cliff face can clearly be seen, even in a monochrome photograph. Huddled in their deckchairs to escape the wind, only the intrepid few are braving the water on this particular day.

Opposite above: The Green, Hunstanton 1921 (71020) Nannies and their charges are all engrossed in playtime upon the green. Hunstanton today still has the genteel air of its Victorian origins, with large turreted villas grouped around the green.

Opposite below: The Beach, Hunstanton 1927 (79729) Children seem to be greatly enjoying the opportunity to play safely in shallow waters.

WELLS-NEXT-THE-SEA. Retaining the atmosphere of a working harbour, Wells has also managed to develop as a popular resort. Its wide sweeping beach is typical of the beauty of the Norfolk coastline. Children fish for crabs by the harbour wall and boats in the creeks continue to search for shellfish, as they have for many years.

Right: The Beach, Wells-next-the-Sea 1929 (81990) The 'Bank', that can just be seen on the horizon, was thrown up in the mid 19th century to provide access to the sea through the muddy silt that was threatening to block the harbour. A wide stretch of salt marsh lies between the town and the sea.

Above: Bring In the Cockles, Wells-next-the-Sea 1929 (82003) Weighed down by his obviously successful catch, this fisherman and the rest of the crew are coming ashore heavily laden with their spoils, carried like a milkmaid used to carry milk, on a double yoke. Cockles, in common with other varieties of shellfish, are delicious freshly caught on the North Norfiolk coast.

Above: The Quay, Wells-next-the-Sea c1955 (W48064) The quay is now a mile from the sea beside a creek, reaached by means of a navigable channel. This small sheltered harbour is host to many boats in high summer. Picturesque in setting, the tranquillity of this scene is comparatively recent for it was a busy port in the export of locally produced grain.

Left: Windmill, Cley-next-the-Sea 1933 (85836) In truth, due to silting, Cley is more than a mile from the sea. Cley Marshes were acquired by the Norfolk Naturalists' Trust in 1926, for the area is the natural habitat of many species of birds. The 18th-century windmill is alongside the old quay, forming part of a picture postcard village.

SHERINGHAM. Grown up around an ancient fishing hamlet, and situated between high cliffs, Sheringham became a popular seaside resort in Victorian times, thanks partly to the railway which made it more accessible, when it opened in 1887. Most of the town was built in the late 19th century, often using pebbles from the beach.

Right: Sheringham from the East 1906 (56873) The old houses are gradually being squeezed out by the new ones, as they all huddle togther on steep banks down to the sea. Boarding houses and hotels sprang up to cater for the growing numbers of visitors.

Below: High Street, Sheringham 1921 (70993) These neo-Tudor buildings amply demonstrate the style of 'instant' building that became holiday Norfolk at the turn of the century.

Above: The Beach, Sheringham 1901
(46540) These fishermen were usually
after crabs or lobsters, but sprats were also
in abundance off this shore. Some are
wearing local 'ganseys', thigh length
leather sea boots.

Left: Sheringham 1893 (33311) These
small beached fishing boats are specially
built with a straight keel, great beam and
full bilges. The general tackle of fishing
can be seen around, crab and lobster
pots, buoys and floats, boxes and baskets.
The cottages on the clifftop may
command magnificent views but they are
in a vulnerable position: many have slid
into the sea in the past.

**Overleaf: Fishermen Mending Lobster
Pots, Sheringham 1906** (56879)
Sheringham fishermen were in fierce
competition with their rivals from nearby
Cromer. Suitably protected against the
elements in sou'westers and oilskin
trousers, they pose artfully for the
photographer.

HOLT. A few miles inland from Sheringham, and seven from Cromer, Holt is mainly Georgian in appearance as a great fire destroyed much of the town in the early 18th century, also gutting the church which has been somewhat unsuccessfully rebuilt. Holt is a compact small market town, with some fine Georgian buildings.

Right: High Street, Holt 1896 (37976) The buildings around the market place are colour washed, hard to see in sepia.

Below: Grammar School, Holt 1896 (37983) This school was founded in 1555, by Sir John Gresham, then Lord Mayor of London. Known locally as Gresham's, it became a public school in 1900, among its eminent former pupils in this century was the poet Auden.

Opposite: Holt Hall from the Lake 1896 (37985) A suitably romantic view of the reflections of Holt Hall, gothic mansion built from castle stone.

EAST RUNTON. As with so many of the villages along the north Norfolk coast, East Runton has a wonderful beach with dramatic cliffs, but somewhat perilous bathing due to strong currents and tides. Yet it offered another holiday pastime that was a firm favourite with the Victorians: ever since Darwin had publshed his famous theories on evolution there had been a craze for 'fossicking', rooting around among the rocks and sands searching for fossils.

Right: Beach Entrance, East Runton 1921 (70968) A classic example of 1920s fashions - the cloche hat, long cardigans and overall shape of the clothes could not be from any other time.

Above: Looking East, East Runton 1933 (85828) Riding on horseback along these endlessly sandy beaches with the sound of the surf must be an exhilarating and unforgettable experience.

Left: High Street, East Runton 1921 (70970) The terraced houses of a village often profited from the summer invasions as they let out rooms for bed and breakfast. These children are absorbed and intrigued by the photgrapher.

Opposite below: The Beach, East Runton c1955 (E11036) The beach huts are still much in evidence, and stand forlornly in rows. This scene is remarkably similar to the pre-war photograph above, with the notable exception of the horses.

CROMER. One of the principal holiday resorts on the north Norfolk coast, Cromer boasts good sands and fine cliff walks. Coastal erosion has swept away the part of Cromer which was a sea port, but fishermen still go out from here, in competition with others along the coast. Cromer crabs are justly famous. One of Jane Austen's characters in *Emma* describes it as 'the best of all the sea bathing places.'

Right: The Promenade and Pier, Cromer 1901 (46522) Major development began in the 1890s as the railway links with London and the Midlands were established. The pier dates from this time.

Above: The Promenade, Cromer 1902 (49069) The Promenade runs along behind the beach, with benches placed at intervals for those who wish to sit quietly reading or staring seawards. Along the Promenade were many houses with balustrated balconies, turrets and bay windows overlooking the sea, which lent a suitably Edwardian atmosphere.

Top: The Sands, Cromer 1899 (44485) There seems to be considerable activity at the water's edge with crowds standing watching: the start of a racec? Or the return of the local crabbers with eager buyers ready to purchase direct from the fishermen? **Above: East Cliff, Cromer 1902** (49070) The bathing machines are clustered together, drawn up away from the beach. **Overleaf: Cromer from the Sea 1902** (49059) The medieval church of St Peter and St Paul is an imposing 15th-century Perpendicular building: its tall tower acted as a lighthouse before an actual one was built. particularly in this view across stormy waves.

Opposite: Cromer 1925 (77511) The cliffs at Cromer are 100 to 200 feet high, and often subject to erosion in places. Cromer grew rapidly, only Yarmouth surpassing it in popularity. **Top: Cromer 1933** (85766) Contemplating the feeling of eternity one has when staring out to sea in a place known to have existed before man walked the earth, 'man's best friend' is taking no chances and keeping close to his master. **Above: Cromer 1921** (70943) Cromer has defied the sea with a strong sea wall, but an older town lies beneath the waves. The church in the distance is a treasurehouse, with a wealth of stained glass by Burne Jones.

SANDRINGHAM. The 7,000 acre estate of Sandringham was given to the future King Edward VII on his coming of age in 1861. When still the Prince of Wales, Edward held New Year shooting parties that continue today as a Royal tradition.

Top: West Front, Sandringham House 1927 (79748) The house was originally Georgian, but was replaced by the present one in Jacobean style. Successive generations have altered the gardens, resulting in new plantings as fashions in gardening have changed.
Above: Sandringham House from the Lake c1955 (S58029) The lakes were excavated in the 19th century and in spring are fringed with irises, primulas, and lilies.

Above: Castle Rising 1898 (40896) Built in the 12th century by a Norman family, the d'Albini, this solid castle stands on a high mound, and has a chequered history. In the 14th century, Queen Isabella was imprisoned here by her son for her complicity in the murder of her husband, Edward II.

Left: Castle Rising 1898 (40895) Successive owners of the Castle have included the Black Prince and Richard II who exchanged it with the Duke of Brittany for the castle at Brest. Somehow it was exchanged by Henry VIII with his uncle, Thomas Howard, Duke of Norfolk, and has been in the Howard family ever since, even though it is now adminstered by English Heritage.

WALSINGHAM. By tradition, pilgrims would remove their shoes at the hamlet of Houghton St Giles, and continue barefoot the remaining mile to Walsingham's shrine of the Virgin Mary. In the Middle Ages, the shrine was second only to Becket's tomb at Canterbury as the major objective of Christian pilgrims. Henry VIII walked barefoot to the shrine and is said to have placed a necklace around the neck of the Virgin's statue: this alas did not prevent him from destroying both statue and buildings some years later on the Dissolution of the Monasteries.

Right: Abbey East Window, Walsingham 1929 (82030) In the 12th century, a widow, Richelde de Fervaques, was transported in a dream to Nazareth and shown the Holy House, the scene of the Annunciation, and instructed to build a replica in Walsingham. Some years later, a relative endowed an Augustinian priory to look after the shrine and a successful pilgrimage industry was established.

Above: Pump and Old Houses, Walsingham 1929 (82032) A 16th-century brick conduit stands over a medieval well in the centre of old Walsingham, a fine sight with many timber-framed houses with overhanging storeys. Nowadays the town has a faintly continental air, as many shops are devoted to the sale of religious souvenirs.

Top: Hempton Mill, Fakenham 1922 (71083) A fine example of East Anglian weatherboarding, this mill is just outside Fakenham on the River Wensum. **Above: The River and Bridge, Fakenham 1929** (82022) The River Wensum flows by this pleasant market town, where low-roofed houses and shops crowd around the old church. John of Gaunt was lord of the manor. The trees crowd thickly down to the water, casting their reflections amongst the reeds. In the distance is the old arched bridge. Two children are enjoying a picnic beside the lane.

Above: Market Place, Swaffham 1891
(29103) A beautiful 18th-century market town, Swaffham became fashionable in Regency times. The neighbouring gentry gathered at the Assembly Rooms during the winter. The fine Palladian market cross stands in the centre of the market place surmounted by a figure of Ceres, goddess of plenty, with a sheaf of corn.

Left: Market Place, Swaffham 1891
(29104) Country families would take houses at Swaffham for 'the season' for in addition to the Assembly Rooms, there was a lively theatre which in 1806 was visited by Lord and Lady Nelson, together with their daughter and Lady Hamilton. The thought of all that activity is just a bit too hectic for this sleepy Victorian dog-day afternoon.

EAST DEREHAM. At the very heart of Norfolk, geographically speaking, the name possibly derives from a legend concerning St Withburga who founded a nunnery in AD 654, and survived a famine thanks to the milk of two deer. She was the daughter of Annas, King of the East Angles. A well named after her is in the churchyard.

Right: Old Houses, East Dereham 1898 (42765) It is unusual to see thatch and pargetry in Norfolk, but these cottages are fine examples of both. A row of thatched cottages beside the church, Bishop Bonner's Cottages, survived a disastrous fire in 1581.

Above: Wash Bridge, East Dereham 1893 (33308) The church behind was once at the centre of town but moved west following the 16th-century fire. The poet William Cowper died here in 1800 and is commemorated in a stained glass window in the church. A more recent author, George Borrow, was born here but adopted Norwich as his city. **Overleaf: Market Place, East Dereham 1898** (42757) Travelling fairs were very popular and they would set up on common land or market place, usually at Easter or Bank Holiday time.

NORWICH. The particular character of Norwich owes much to the fact that it has always been an isolated city, cut off from the rest of the country by the Wash and the Fens. It must be remembered that it was a port and it would have been quicker for a Norwich man to sail across to Belgium or Holland than to go to London before the railways came. With a Norman castle and the finest cathedral in East Anglia, it is indeed Norfolk's capital city.

Right: Elm Hill, Norwich 1929 (81805) This cobbled street has been preserved today, with little alteration. Antique dealers line it, much the same as in this photograph. At the centre of Norwich are narrow streets and winding alley ways with overhanging houses, giving it a unique appeal.

Below: Bishopsgate Street, Norwich 1921 (70881) Bishopsgate Street leads to Bishop's Bridge which was built in 1295 by the prior of Norwich. A centre for agricultural equipment, mustard, boots and shoes and silk-weaving.

Top: Royal Hotel and Post Office, Norwich 1901 (46672) Known as a centre for agricultural equipment, the manufacture of mustard, leather boots and shoes and also for silk-weaving, established by the Huguenots in the 17th century, Norwich was a thriving industrial and trading city. **Above: Norwich from St James's Hill 1896** (37342) It is said of Norwich that there is 'a church for every week; a pub for every day'. This overall panoramic view takes in a few of those towers and spires but the pubs are harder to spot. **Overleaf: Rampant Horse Street, Norwich 1891** (28163) Colman's Mustard is made at the end of King Street at Carrow Works.

Right: Thorpe Reach, Norwich 1899
(44478) This scene although
photographed in the 1890s could
equally be a watercolour from the
Norwich School of Painting.
Founded by John Crome in the early
19th century and famous
throughout Europe, to some extent
Crome and Cotman anticipated
Impressionist ideas, to convey the
essence of a subject rather than an
exact reproduction. Examples of
their work are in the Castle Museum
in Norwich.

Above: Yacht Station, Norwich 1938 (88656) There is boating on the river Yare which goes around Norwich, and is joined by the river
Wensum. Norwich's early wealth was based on wool, exported to the markets of the Low Countries via these two rivers to the sea.
Opposite: River, Thorpe, Norwich 1919 (69075)

Right: Cow Tower, Norwich 1896 (37364)
The ruins of one of the old city towers, the
Cow Tower, are on the river Wensum, on
the fringe of the city. It was rebuilt in brick
on its original stone foundations at the end
of the 14th century.

**Below: From above Pull's Ferry, Norwich
1896** (37343) The river runs half round the
city, busy with shipping and pleasure boats,
and crossed by a dozen or so bridges. Pull's
Ferry was in fact a bridge, and water gate,
built of flint 500 years ago to guard the
river approach to the cathedral.

Opposite: Norwich Cathedral 1930 (85099)
The Norman Cathedral is one of the jewels
of the whole of East Anglia, not only of
Norwich. The interior contains some of the
finest carved stone bosses, carved
misericords and stained glass in the
country. Only Salisbury has a higher spire.
On top of the spire, some 315 feet from the
ground, was a golden chanticleer.

NORFOLK BROADS. Broadland is a place justly famed for its tranquil beauty. The early Victorian amateur sailors and enthusiasts do not know what they began: today nearly a quarter of a million people take boating holidays here. As a result the ecology is threatened. The rivers form the framework of 125 miles of navigable waterway. The combination of marshes, water and sky is an enduring image of the wide open and windswept landscapes of East Anglia.

Right: The Broads and River Bure, Salhouse 1902 (48143) Some five miles south-east of Norwich, Salhouse is on the river Bure, close to the Bure Marshes. Water lilies used to cover Salhouse Broad. Great Hoveton Broad is nearby.

Above: The Broads, Salhouse 1902 (48144) The reeds and marshes of the Broads are perfect breeding grounds and camouflage for a rich variety of water birds. The old-fashioned sailing barges with their dark crimson sails gliding past the reeds could be straight out of a Dutch old master painting. **Opposite above: Mill and River, The Broads c1934** (T213064) Windmills and low, hump-back bridges and weatherboarded mills are typical of the Broads. **Opposite below: The Village, Coltishall 1902** (48166)

Right: River Steamer, Acle c1929
A204034) Even in the 1920s a boat trip on a steamer was often crowded, as can be seen by its low waterline in the river. The fishermen fish on quite unperturbed.

Below: The River and River Walk, Acle 1929 (A204030) Broadland was a quiet world of water and wildlife until Victorian sailing enthusiasts began arriving in their relentless search for somewhere new and different. Already by the 1920s motor cruisers were in use, and it is the motor that sadly is damaging the natural balance of Broadland.

Above: View from Acle Bridge c1929 (A204024) Wooden hulled yachts line the banks of the Bure. Boating in the Twenties was slow and unhurried. It also had its own dress code, of baggy trousers and yachting cap. Acle is now a large marina on the river Bure, some eight miles west of Great Yarmouth.

Left: The Green from the Post Office, Acle c1926 (A204004) The keen sailors would have to go ashore for their supplies. In the Twenties they would have found a still unspoiled rural village.

Above: On the Thurne, Potter Heigham c1926 (P167040) Potter Heigham is at the centre of the Broads boating industry. The medieval bridge which crosses the Thurne has extremely low headroom and yachts have to lower their masts to pass beneath: a sign warning CAUTION is prominent on the bridge. This couple in their sleek motor launch would pass through easily.

Left: River Thurne, Potter Heigham 1934 (86382) The Thurne is a tributary of the Bure, running through flatter open marshland. Much of the area is below sea level. The wind-pumps that today no longer drain the maze of dykes still retain their old sail arms.

Opposite above: Sunset Punt Ferry, The Broads c1934 (T213074) A punt was one of the many forms of boating enjoyed before the motor completely took over the waterways of the Broads, and an ideal way to watch the bird life without disturbing them unduly.

Opposite below: Fleet Dyke, The Broads c1934 (T213091) The perfect end to a day, sailing home into the sunset on an almost deserted stretch of water.

Above: The Evening Ferry, The Broads c1934
(T213073) If lucky, the bird life to be seen on
the Broads can include many different kinds of
warblers, flycatchers, kestrels and marsh
harriers and the occasional rare bittern.

Left: Station Road, Wroxham 1921 (70891)
Wroxham is also on the river Bure, with a long
sheet of water known as Wroxham Broad
where sailing boats can potter or race with
more space than on the river itself. These
commercial opportunists are proudly offering
Motor Boats for Hire and one is suitably
smartly dressed for the occasion in blazer and
yachting cap.

Opposite above: Wroxham Broad 1934
(86359) Spectator sport for this lady who is
wearing her sensible sunhat as she watches the
activities of the yachts out upon the Broad.

Opposite below: The Village, Wroxham 1921
(70890) The unofficial capital of the Broads,
Wroxham is often a starting point for
excursions further into the maze of waterways.
Traffic is infrequent enough to allow a stall to
set up in the middle of the street, watched idly
by a group outside the village stores.

GREAT YARMOUTH. Still a busy working fishing port, Yarmouth is an important herring-fishing port. A mixture of ancient and modern, holiday and work, it suffered considerable bomb damage in the Second World War, and many of the ancient narrow alley ways called Rows were lost. The late Victorian holiday resort is at the east, facing the sea, and the modern port is to the south. The main part of the town is built on a sand spit facing the river Yare, not the sea, which flows parallel with the coast, entering the sea at Gorleston.

Right: Wellington Gardens and Pier, Great Yarmouth 1904 (52338) The late Victorian sea front clusters around Wellington Pier. These gardens are close to the pier and provide an elegant setting for the flowing robes of these Edwardian ladies, no doubt staying at one of the nearby grand hotels. Some of these survived the bombing during the last War.

Above: The Promenade and Beach, Great Yarmouth 1908 (60643) The Pier can be seen in the distance, and despite the tramlines, horse transport was still in use. **Opposite: The Promenade, Great Yarmouth 1908** (60646) Increasingly popular, Yarmouth became known as a resort for jolly cockneys wearing paper hats. The gracious and spacious elegance of Edwardian Yarmouth is a marked contrast to bustling crowds and traffic today.

Above: The Promenade and Beach, Great Yarmouth 1894 (33386) Donkey rides and carriages complement an otherwise mainly pedestrian seaside atmosphere. It was the done thing to be tidily dressed, complete with hat or even parasol.

Left: Britannia Pier, Great Yarmouth 1894 (33385) Carriages wait for passengers alongside the second of Yarmouth's piers.

Opposite above: Town Hall, Great Yarmouth 1891 (G56501) The Queen Anne style Town Hall dates only from 1882, but clearly emulates earlier Dutch gabled architecture.

Opposite below: Town Hall, Great Yarmouth 1922 (72536) The paddle steamer moored here would probably be going up and down the coast, running trips to and from Felixstowe, Lowestoft or further afield.

Right: Blackfriars Tower, Great Yarmouth 1891 (28710) A fine old structure of decorative flint work.

Below: The Jetty, Great Yarmouth 1908 (60648) Horse-drawn omnibuses are lined up awaiting customers.

Opposite: The Market, Great Yarmouth 1891 (28716) A sea of awnings stretches out across the broad market square. The aisles are thronged with bargain hunters. In the background, the central tower and spire of the Parish Church rise over the rooftops.

Overleaf: The Quay, Great Yarmouth 1908 (60652) Two men are high up a ladder repairing the street light. The horse-drawn omnibuses are filling up rapidly for excursions along the Promenade. On the right is the Star Hotel.

Index